Critters
An' Calamities

Linda Nadon

To order additional copies of this book, contact:
Xlibris
844-714-8691
www.Xlibris.com
Orders@Xlibris.com

ISBN: Softcover   978-1-6698-1650-8
        EBook   978-1-6698-1649-2

Print information available on the last page

Rev. date: 06/03/2022

Table of Contents

CRITTERS

CALAMITIES

OUTSIDE THE BOX

CRITTERS

Choco, Amigo, Duke, Kruz, Daisy, Wiley, Rowdy and Charm

A Quarter of a Century

Our Lacey is home for Easter, her third year of College is almost at an end.
She heads out to visit the horses to spend some time with her old equine friend

He's a solid little fella, beautiful dark bay with jet black flowing tail and mane
Once a chuck wagon pony, barely 14 hands high, but a heck of a Ranch Horse just the same

We got him when they were both five and they made such a striking pair
The dancing little dark bay pony and the tiny girl with the long golden hair

They always rode at the back any time we moved the cow herds
Prince and Kippie* kept 'em movin' while little Lacey enjoyed the butterflies and birds

He was as good as any big Ranch horse when it was branding time
Prince loved to drag the calves to the irons, as a rope horse he really did shine

And He was an awesome gymkhana pony, quite different when the horn would blast
Our little Prince was a fierce competitor and he was wicked fast

I recall the time Prince and Lacey led the Parade at the Trail rider's Rodeo
He pranced and danced, side passed and even reared Man, they sure put on a show

He's there in her Graduation pictures, in fact, he shared her Wedding Day
She sat upon his back in her white crushed taffeta, She wouldn't have it any other way

Now, I watch from a distance and take a mental picture so it will forever last
Arms around his neck, her golden waves against his jet black mane in such a sharp contrast

For her, her whole life is before her, there's no end to possibilities that lie ahead
For him, his best days are behind him, the day is coming that we all dread

They are standing quietly together, sharing 20 years of memories untold
The sway-backed old pony and our beautiful young daughter, both a quarter of century old

*Kippie (pictured on the front cover) was my first cattle dog. She was a border collie and she was my partner for 12 years. I'v had a few dogs since but she will always have a special place in my heart.

March 2013

The Ol' Boys

The ol' boys are out to pasture, their workin' days are done
soakin' up the warm winter rays, standin' broadside to the sun

they spend their days together, unaware of life's fast pace
content to watch the world go by, they've already run their race

Bud was the neighbor girl's barrel horse. He was the "all around" kind
On the trail, team roping, or working cattle, horses like Bud are hard to find

They made us proud Bud and Rae-Lee, but now she's a mother and a wife
Chasing two youngsters fills up her days, she's moved on with her life

And Prince was our Lacey's Ranch horse another good one that's for sure
And for nearly a quarter of a century, he was more than a horse to her.

Her best friend since she was 5, the best horse a girl could want
He shared all her growing pains of youth, he was her confidante

Now our Lacey lives in the city, movin' up the ranks with Mary Kaye
Driving the car, living the life, in a world so far away

If they make it thru this winter, they'll be 30 in the spring
But, one just can't predict what Old Man Winter will bring

Survivors of another life when we were in our prime
Remnants of a memory, a world, a place, a time.

December 2017

Ode to my Cutting Horse (Revised)

It's springtime again we was pickin' an' choosin'
Which heifers was winnin' and which ones was losin'

I thought we must-a had all the best ones picked out
When My Larry started to have just a shadow of a doubt

And he says to me "you know that ol' number one-ten"?
She's a good'un, WE best cut her daughter outta that pen.

I know just how busy my Larry can be
And when he say's "we" it most likely means "me"

I looked at all of them yearlin's figured I'd be needin' some luck"
He wanted me to pull one heifer outta that pen full of muck

Well, it didn't take me a whole lotta time to decide
If I's gonna do any <u>cut</u>tin', I was sure gonna ride

So, I saddled up my Rebel and rode into that pen
In no time at all we spotted heifer number one-ten

And we went at it kinda easy and slow
And we got her cut out, and wouldn't you know

All I did was hang on and it didn't take long
my mount didn't falter never made one move wrong

Yup, he'd sure enough figured out what I wanted
Tho' the footin' was poor my mount was undaunted

I patted his neck and said "Man, that was fun
you shore are a cow-cuttin' son of a gun"

He's a real cuttin' pony, He's shore got the knack
He knows a lot more than the dumb blonde on his back.

This is one of my first poems. The first version contained way too many slant rhymes as I knew nothing of rhyme and metre.

A Ranch Horse and a Real Good Dog

The best thing about raisin' cattle is that I get to ride
All I need is a good Ranch Horse and my cattle dog by my side

With my Tippie keepin' 'em movin', and me a-ridin' the wing
We can put 'em right where we want 'em, we can do most anything

If you've never had a real good dog, I truly feel sorry for you
I'd take a dog over them wanna-be cowboys who really don't have a clue

These cattle dogs are smart and they work on instinct without being told
A real good dog is pretty well priceless they're worth their weight in gold

And I got me some real fine Ranch horses that I would trade for none
Always willin' to go where I ask, always willin' to get the job done

They plough thru' thick trees and willows, over dead fall and even brush piles
No matter how tough the terrain, no matter how many the miles

They wade the creeks, they swim the rivers, they wallow thru' swamp and mud bog
I reckon I got all the help that I need with a Ranch Horse and a real good dog

August 2016

Ben (Larry's horse), Patty (Landon's first Horse), Slim (My horse) All sadly missed!

My Morgan Mares Daisy and Charm.

Rowdy pulling me on the stoneboat.

Replacin' Ben

We lost 'ol Ben on a cold winter's night quite some years ago
Reckon he died of a heart attack, there was no sign of struggle in the snow

It all but broke my Larry's heart 'cause he really loved his Ben
And I had to find a replacement tho' I didn't know how or when

Ben was only 18 but he'd been Larry's saddle horse for nigh onto 13 years
And not bein' able to replace him was one of my greatest fears

He was only 14-1 but he was solid, and he was awesome in the ropin' pen
And we never worried about the kids when they were ridin' Ben

When it came to our youngest, Landon, we could trust Ben in any circumstance
But, with Larry it was a different story, 'cause he'd buck if he got the chance

Especially on them frosty fall roundups, We'd kinda hang back to watch the show
We'd all wait 'til Larry was mounted, You never knew when Ben was gonna blow

Ben wasn't really dirty, and Larry figured they got along just fine
'Cause as long as he paid attention, Ben would never step out of line

I rarely rode Ben, he was rough gaited and hard mouthed, but that horse sure could track
Put him on a cow and he'd never come off, he'd chase her to Hell and back

He'd set you up perfect, every time, right in that real sweet spot
Then his ears would go back as if to say "You gonna throw that rope or not?"

Ben was a no nonsense kind of horse. You could count on him to get the job done
The crew still misses the rodeos and the cold mornin's ain't quite as much fun

Larry's new mount, Choco, is a smooth movin' geldin' he's nice'n light in the mouth too
I'm thinkin', maybe Larry doesn't miss Ben quite as much as the rest of us do

Ben (Larry's Horse), Patty (Landon's first Horse) and Slim (Linda's Horse) all sadly missed!

Daisy Mae

Today I rode my Daisy Mae across the deep white snow
Not without some trepidation, wasn't sure how she would go

She's supposed to be saddle broke but hadn't been rode in years
A familiar horse-dealin' story, hence, the reason for my fears

And I ain't quite as brave as when I was a younger hand
Hence, the nice deep snow, a much safer place to land

She's a 10-yr old black Morgan mare and I bought her for a song
She's got a real sweet disposition, just seems to want to get along

I stood up on the trailer and she sidled up beside
So I could mount with ease, seemed eager to get on with our ride

She ain't no neck reiner, straight reinin' is all she knows
But, she stays between yer knees and when you ask, she whoas

We headed out on our adventure and when she broke into a trot
It was like ridin' on a cloud and I remembered why I bought

This gaited mare, I really thought I'd died and went to heaven
Looks like yer a keeper, Daisy Mae, welcome to the N7

January 5, 2021

Rowdy

Today I finally got the chance to make my solo run
Filled with anticipation, it was gonna be such fun

The harness was just a pile of buckles, rings and snaps
Hames and chains and tugs and many other leather straps

Bill had been real thorough when he had "walked" me thru' it
But now that I was on my own, I weren't sure that I could do it

Rowdy stood there calmly as It took a couple tries
I'm not real sure, but I swear, I seen him roll his eyes

If patience is a virtue, My Rowdy is a Saint
He's 16-2, I'm 4 foot 10 and I'm afraid I cain't

Reach that big brute from the ground, I needed to be taller
He bowed his neck and dropped his head and I slipped on his Collar

I stood on a molasses tub to throw the harness o'er his back
Buckled the hames into the collar, Hey! I think I've got the knack

It was time for the bridle, once again he dropped his head
I almost cried, for this was the part that filled my heart with dread

I finished with the harness hooked up to the single tree
That Bill gave me for the stone boat the "my Larry" made for me

And off we went across the snow, I felt like I was in heaven
Rowdy, my gentle giant gem, welcome to the N7

February 27, 2021

Bill Rempel is a close neighbour and friend who came over to help me with my new venture.

Kruz

He shore was a big strong young'un, that cremello we called Kruz
Comin' 6 this Spring, such potential, the kind you hate to lose

He shore could cover ground, he was a fast walkin', smooth movin' brute
A mud-boggin, bush wackin' heck of a mount and "bomb proof" to boot

We rode for miles in the lease last summer thru' willows, brush and trees
He never seemed to slow his pace and he NEVER smashed my knees

Shelby rode him on the trail ride tho' she only rides once a year
He was stellar never once stepped out of line, I had no need to fear

He'd been in more than a few wrecks but I always doctored him thru'
But, Kruz, this time Dr. Winchester was the only choice left for you

Yup! He shore would'a been a dandy, that big horse we called Kruz
Comin' 6 this Spring, so much potential, the kind you hate to lose

January 25, 2022

Ode to Ol' 139

When I made the dusk patrol last night, this is what I found
Ol' one-thirty-nine's new calvie had arrived safe and sound

She was born in 2001 had her first calf in 2003
And every calf she's blessed us with was delivered trouble free

This one's a sturdy little girlie, she must weigh at least one-ten
No doubt this time next year she'll be in the replacement pen

Her mom's a big ol' bossy, she shows a lot of Simmental
She'll raise one of our top calves and come in slick and fat this fall

I reckon her daddy's a Gelbvieh she's big boned and golden red
If it's hybrid vigour you're lookin' for, this little one is very well bred

The advice now-a-days is to keep your heifers off of the younger stock
They have "superior genetics" they say, I say that's just a crock

We prefer to build our herd from Moms who have proven their worth over time
Calvin' time would be so much easier If the whole herd was like ol' one-thirty-nine.

May 2015

Ol' 139 (the sequel)

When I checked the cows one mornin', this is what I found
Ol' one-thirty-nine's new calvie was up and runnin' 'round

This one's a big-boned burly bully, He surely is a brute
with his gangly gait and spotted face, He's awkward but he's cute

He's a lucky little feller, He's got one of our best mothers
He'll be one of our biggest steers this fall just like all her others

We're barely 10 days into calvin' I think this calf makes 72
This ol' gal calves way earlier than a lot of them younger cows do

I was lookin' through my records, and much to my surprise
I found she'd had a set of twins back in 2005

Her first calf was born in 2003, so, I guess this one makes 15
I tell you, cows like Ol' one-thirty-nine, they're few and far between

April 2016

Ol' Three Tags

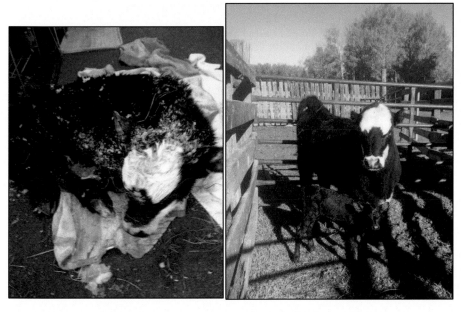

Face   *The little Brockle-Face*

Ol' Three Tags

We were sortin' cows today, I had a lump in my throat
As I turned her in with the culls and this is the poem I wrote

It was the fall of 2010, we had a bumper crop of hay
the supply exceeded demand, so you could barely give it away

Well, "My Larry" and I was ponderin' just what we should do
We decided to by some "one-calf cows" to put all that hay through

So, we bought 65 bred cows and she was in that pack
We, gave them all an N7 tag just so we could keep track

she already had two tags, so the one we gave her made three
we always called her "Ol' Three Tags" though her number was nine-forty-three

She's a dark red white- faced cow and actually she's quite small
Deep-bodied her belly is close to the ground she's hardly got legs at all

She's got really thick lashes like the cookie monster on Sesame Street
And not unlike Big Bird, she really has big feet

She has a pointed head but her offspring often have horns
she was likely cosmetically dehorned, not polled when she was born

She delivered her 10th calf on our Ranch a couple weeks ago
How many she'd had before that, I guess we'll never know

She was not young when we got her I reckon this calf will be her last
'cause just like dogs and horses, cows also get old too fast

Yeah, I know she's just a cow, but she's kinda special to me
My little "cookie monster cow","Ol' Three Tags", number nine-forty-three

The Little Black Brockle-Faced Cow

Born on Valentine's day, not the gift I was hopin' for
A half-froze newborn heifer calf dumped on my kitchen floor

Her momma was a bred cow that we had recently bought
marked to calf in April or May at least that's what we thought

Next spring, I was doin' chores, pullin' twines off of the hay
Shore enough she was baggin' up, ready to calf right away

She was 15 months old, was on pasture when she got bred
knowin' she was out with the "big bulls" filled my heart with dread

she delivered a tiny black calf with no help at all
he was near as big as his momma when we weaned that fall

we wintered her with the heifers and when she calved again
She was smaller than the first-calvers that were in that pen

we preg-checked the cows that fall, I held my breath just hopin'
she would be in calf again, of course, SHE wasn't open*

"My Larry" said if she was dry* we'd keep her anyway
'Cause she's still one calf ahead, she's already paid her way

Spring 2018

A cow that is not pregnant (in calf) is said to be "dry" or "open"

Hang in there Girls!

I'm surveyin' the cow herd and it's lookin' kinda scary
'Cause Old Man Winter ain't been kind here in mid-February

The nights are near the -30 mark, fact it's been down right harsh
And we went and bought some cows that are due to calf in March

Seemed like a good deal at the time, now it sure does not
Shouldn't be no calves 'til April, except this bunch we bought

Don't be in a hurry girls, this cold snap won't last too long
It's gonna warm up soon, hope that weather man ain't wrong

Two weeks later . . . .

I'm scrutinizin' backends and I'm analizin' bags
Doin' my "due diligence" checkin' all the tags

I'm searchin' fer that white-tailed cow, she ain't too hard to spot
Reckon she's my favourite of the bunch that we just bought

There she is, I see her now, I'm a thinkin' she might be first
Hang in there girl, a few more days and we'll be thru' the worst

When it comes to calvin' ,it's anybody's guess
It's just this dang cold weather that is causin' me duress

'course these ol' gals can fool you, she may well be the last
Some cows show forever, while others come on fast

Our son's been thinkin' that maybe we should buy some more
It's fine with me but they better be wearin' number four*

When the vet pregnancy checks the cows, he writes the number of the month the calf is expected on the cow's hip. #4 would be April

Weanin' Time

It really is a ruckus list'nin' to the calvies bawl
The mounful weanin' song we are blessed with every fall

the cows and calves are separated each year when we wean
I feel bad for all the critters, it seems kinda mean

They are no longer babies, they're 6 or 7 months by now
Momma's got a new one comin', gotta think about the cow

Bovines are so domesticated what are we to do
She won't wean on her own, gotta think 'bout the new calf too

She can't feed all three of them and maintain her condition
Thru' the long cold winter up to her next parturition

Momma cows are quite prolific, they are downright amazin'
Lactatin' and gestatin' while they are calmly grazin'

When we take her big suckin' calf, perhaps it's a relief
In a few short days, Momma cow forgets about her grief

It's really kinda sad list'nin' to their mournful song
One thing is for certain, they won't bawl for very long

November 2021

Canine Infantry

I should've brought a horse, I really should've known
But it was -33 and a cold North wind was blowin'

The plan was simple "My Larry" in the bale truck drivin' in the lead
And me, followin' in my pick-up, the cows should follow the feed

Winter had struck with a vengeance what could possibly go wrong
We was only a mile and a half from home, shouldn't take too long

And once we got'em out the gate there were fences on each side
The cows should just head for home, there'd be no need to ride

This was a fool proof plan, should work without a hitch
But, even the best made plans often have a glitch

Larry couldn't cross the creek, because it was too rough
And when I'd fed the day before, I'd fed more than enough

The cows did not want to leave, they were quite content
Clearly, they had not received the memo that I sent

I could not make them move, sittin' there inside my truck
If I was on my horse, I'd a had much better luck

But, I had a secret weapon ridin' "shotgun" next to me
I'd brought my cattle dog "Tippie" along, my canine infantry.

December 2017

Boss & Spike

It was a sad day when young Sadie Brooks met her untimely demise
Orphaned were eight 12-day old puppies that had barely opened their eyes.

It surely was a dilemma all them puppies was needin' a mother
Landon came home with Boss and I sent him back for another

I knew if I had two, they would be much more content
I'd raise them both and give Spike away, that was my intent

But they are my "boys" I just couldn't give my Spikey away
They're almost like my children so they're both here to stay

Sadie was a blue heeler, so our "boys" have cow dog breedin'
And they earn their keep watchin' gates all winter when we're feedin'

And how they love to "move em", ya don't have to tell 'em twice
Now, if callin' em off was as easy, that would really be nice

No, they ain't no border collie, They truly lack finesse
The fine art of workin' cattle they do not posess

But when you got an ornery bull that won't cooperate
My "boys" only gotta heel 'im once and he's lookin' for the gate

And it shore don't take 'em long to break up a bull fight
Them bulls are lookin' to escape, it only takes one bite

They are not at all the same, they are as different as day and night
Boss kinda' looks like a Rottweiler and Spike is almost white

Boss is a big bafoon, Spike has a serious side
And there's nothing they enjoy more than to go for a buggy ride

Yes, they are my "boys" they are part of the family
My constant, loyal companions, they mean the world to me

2014

My Boss Boy

You're gettin' old my Boss Boy, you can't smell or hear or see
But you can feel the love in the touch of my hand and you live to be with me

Your brother Spike is faring better he's rather portly but still quite spry
He's got no real health issues, except for the "old dog" sore on his eye

When you were just a young'un, you were caught in a power snare
you are payin' for it now, it's almost more than I can bear

but it truly is a miracle that you managed to survive
that snare failed, caught you by the waist, and that's why you're alive

Now, you're gettin' weak in the back end and you struggle to get up
I remember when you lost your mama you were a 12-day-old pup

I bottle fed you and your brother and you both grew up big and strong
You boys will be 13 in the spring, it doesn't seem like that long

That you've been helpin' with the chores, the guarder of the gate
You never left your post no matter how long you had to wait

Down the driveway I'd go to the hay yard to get another bale
When I returned, I could count on you to be there without fail

And it wasn't just the gates, that you loved to guard
Perched atop a hay bale, you kept vigil on your yard

I pray when you cross the Rainbow Bridge, you'll do it on your own
But I promise that you'll not suffer and you won't be alone

When you take your final breath, Boss Boy, I'll be there with you
For you've been my faithful companion, It's the least that I can do.

January 26, 2022

Amigo

When I've got some cattle work to do and I'm choosin' from the cavy
I'll probably pick my paint 'cause he's got the most cow savvy

I bought him as a 3-yr old and he was pretty green
was s'posed to be a kid's horse, but his boy was not so keen

I felt bad for the boy, but, for me it was pure luck
Then, I found he was kinda broncy, fact, he was prone to buck

I used a short shanked swivel bit so he couldn't get his head
And he never did buck me off but if it was now-a-days instead

I'd just turn him in circles so he couldn't dump me on the ground
The new way to end a problem is to turn them round and round

I didn't do much whisperin' my method's were "old School"
My claim is not a horse trainer, but, he's a real cow cuttin' fool

I reckon he's a fine Ranch Horse, but when I list his Pro's and Con's
The Pro side is kinda short but the Con side, well, it's rather long

He ain't the lightest reinin' horse but when we's workin' cattle
You'll be scratchin' leather just to stay there in the saddle

he's just a tad lazy, but this is not always bad
'Cause if he let's one past him, it sure does make him mad

He know's he'll have to run 'em down, if he let's 'em by
So, he seldom misses, he's got no end to try

He ain't real fast but he gets me there, so I guess he's fast enough
And he ain't the smoothest gaited horse, in fact, he's down right rough

Yup! The pro side is kinda scarce while the con side is kinda full
But, by gosh, let me tell you that paint can work a bull
I
And for you folks who don't think this is a worthy attribute
I reckon you've never had to work a half-crazed bovine brute

CALAMITIES

Vet. Techin'

When it comes to treatin' the ailin', on our Ranch that job is all mine
And since I'm a Vet. Tech. by trade, that usually suits me jest fine

I treat for scours and pneumonia for bloat, lump jaw and foot rot
don't get to do much fancy vet techin' don't get to practice the skills I was taught

Well, today we had a calf that was strainin', don't worry, I know what to do
Even tho' I haven't done this procedure in at least a decade or two

My Tippie, brought him up the alley and I caught him in the head lock,
I pushed it all in and it kept on a-comin' out, reckon he'll need a spinal block,

I hit the target first try, injected the freezing, his tail went limp and numb
I cleaned things up, the best I could, then shoved it all back where it had come from

I then performed the "draw-string", It's been years since I've done one of those
and I finished it off with a flourish, two knots and the neatest of bows

So, if you're ever in need of assistance, jest call me, I might even come
'Cause I reckon I'm right up there with the best at repairin' a prolapsed Rectum!!!!!

April 2016

By Chance (or Dug-out Disaster)

It was calvin' time, I was watchin' the cows they were content just eatin' their hay
Some calvies were snugglin' in for a nap, some calvies wanted to play

I noticed a cow break from the herd, I guessed she wanted to be alone
I reckoned it wouldn't be very long 'fore she had a wee calf of her own

Then, I watched as she started to deliver she'd chose the worst possible spot
That's no place for a calf to be born, or at least, that's what I thought

On top of the dirt pile surroundin' the dug-out, there's no way this calf could win
If he goes North he's in the swamp, If he goes South, he best know how to swim

I hate to interfere, but, I just could not leave this to fate
I went over to make her move but, I arrived a moment too late

He was born and slid into the water, His lungs never even filled up with air
I knew if I didn't act quickly, that calf was gonna drown in there

I took a moment to call for help, Thank God I had my cell phone
that dugout was deep in places, I thought it not wise to do this alone

Then, I dived into the frigid water, swam to where the calf disappeared
It was way colder than I was prepared for, but not near as deep as I feared

I grabbed ahold, dragged him to the edge, he was so slimy and wet
Now, Mama Cow's tryin' to kill me, She's decided that I am the threat

The calf was strugglin' and gaspin' for breath, I was desperately tryin' to hang on
Suddenly, He broke free from my grasp, in an instant he was gone

I was frozen and pretty well done for, just as Landon and Larry arrived
If they'd come a moment later, that calf would have never survived

It's by chance that I chose to linger and not just go on my way
And It's by chance that I was there to save that little calvie that day

April 2016

Runaway Rig

I was checkin' the cows at dusk, I could'a spotted him from a mile
ears hangin', eyes sunk in looked like he hadn't sucked in a quite awhile

I loaded him on the floor of my buggy, figured I'd bring him in for the night
I'd treat him for scours and pneumonia and tube him with electrolyte

Well, it was a real bad decision when I stepped off to open the gate
The calf struggled, pressed on the gas, and away he sped straight

for the dug out at the speed of sound wildly doing the zag and the zig
That dogie had'er in the big wheel I'd never catch that run-away rig

They hit a hole, heaven help us, now they're a-circlin' 'round to the right
looks like they're gonna miss the dug-out, I prayed with all my might

Now, they're careenin' thru' the herd, cattle leapin' out of the way
things was goin' from bad to worse, I just continued to pray

Finally, the buggy started to slow down, the calf had shifted his weight
I caught up, gained control and avoided a disastrous fate

So, I guess I've learned my lesson, when a calvie is ridin' with me,
I will not leave that buggy, until I've turned off the key.

March 2017

Ain't got no Leg to Stand On

I hobbled o'er to the thermometer and it said minus one
Now, I'm layin' here a-ponderin' the things that should get done

But, there ain't nothin' gonna happen and it's dang near killin' me
'Cause there's nothin' I can do, now that I've gone and wrecked my knee
But, lay here on the couch with my crutches next to me

I've had some time to do some thinkin' as I while away my days
This new injury's brought new meanin' to that old familiar phrase

"She ain't got a leg to stand on" seems to fit my situation
This time I've wrecked my "good" knee which adds to my limitation
Not knowin' which knee hurts the worse can cause great irritation

It might not be quite so bad, if this were somethin' new
But, I was holdin' down the couch at this same time last year too

A dang cow kicked me in my "bad" knee, it's worse than it was before
Now, it seems I got two "bad" knees ain't got no "good" knee anymore

I better mind my "P's" and "Q's" better listen to the Doc.
Better give this knee a chance to heal, don't do what I aught not
Or, I won't have one good leg to stand on and that's a scary thought

So, I guess I'll just hold down the couch, I ain't gonna moan
I'll read some cowboy poetry - maybe write some of my own.

Feb. 2015

Knot Pretty

My gorgeous palomino has a knot in his flaxen mane
I know this kind of travesty could drive most "horse" folks insane

but, here in the Great White North, I will often just ride bareback
The warmth from my horse feels way better than all that frozen tack

Most times I don't even use a bridle just a halter and a lead
We always get where we're goin' so I guess that's all we need

And My Wiley is 15-1, it's a long way to the ground
So, when I'm slowly slidin' off his back, that knot, I have found

Is a godsend, I grab ahold and then carefully I ease
My ol' body to the ground so much better for my knees

You may call my horses neglected, but do not judge so quick
A curried mane might be pretty but, that knot sure does the trick

Mountin' Up

To all of you tall, long, lanky cowboys, I reckon you just don't understand
What it's like to be vertically challenged, to stand less than 15 hands

I never made the 5 foot club, tho', on my Driver's licence, I lied
I wish I could just swing into the saddle and merrily go for a ride

If you was ever to visit our Ranch and just take a look around,
You'll find a block or a pail at every gate 'cause I can't mount from the ground

All my horses are real accommodatin', I step up and they sidle up real close
And they don't move 'til I'm set in the saddle, they stand just like a post

You see, I totally wrecked my right knee playing college basketball
Don't laugh! I was a mighty fine player even tho' I'm not very tall

So doin' that hop thing to get my foot in the stirrup, it just doesn't work for me
'Cause you got to be able to bounce and there ain't no bounce in my knee

It's definitely not fair that stirrup length is inversely proportional to height
The taller the rider the longer the stirrup, now to me that don't seem right

When you're not tall like me, the stirrup ain't very long, so what's a cowgal to do
When your stirrup is up near your chin and that's on my horse that's 14-2

Next time you step into your stirrup, don't look at us short folk with scorn. Instead,
you might consider givin' a leg up to those of us who can't even reach the horn

October 2012

Three-legged Horses

I reckon horses should be three-legged, that would be just great for me
'cause when it comes to clippin' hooves, I'm only good for three

The first two trim up easy, but the third one is gettin' tough
And by the time I'm finished, I've really had enough

But, you just can't turn 'em loose with all hooves clipped but one
You've just gotta "cowboy up" and get that fourth one done

It's gettin' ever harder as the years go by
I've hired it done a couple of times, but I'm hard to satisfy

You can't just clip the wall, sometimes ya gotta trim the sole
I like a round rasped finish, you know "the mustang roll"

A farrier can trim up the whole herd in an hour or two
if I trim all them hooves myself, It takes days to do

But, I've come up with a solution that I think will suit me fine
And I'll get them done the way I want, I'll just do them two at a time

Spring 2018

Muck Hole

We live and work in a muck hole, there ain't too much can be done
When spring winds are blowin' and snow is goin' and water is startin' to run

We live and work in a muck hole, while other folks pray for rain
We pray for dry ground, but there's none to be found, dry landers must think we're insane

We live and work in a muck hole, there's a lake at ev'ry gate
'Cause the water will flow to the place that is low and wet feet is one thing that I hate

We live and work in a muck hole, the mid-day sun is sure pleasin'
Then it drops outta sight, and we're up checkin' all night to save newborn calvies from freezin'

We live and work in a muck hole, where the wind cuts right thru' your hide
If you don't like to be froze, don't choose the life that I've chose, you likely won't enjoy the ride

We live and work in a muck hole, when the grass finally starts to grow
Old Man Winter strikes back and he cuts us no slack, he buries that new grass in snow.

We live and work in a muck hole, but, once we've made it to the spring
Pastures turn lush, grass where once there was mush we rejoice in what summer will bring!!

We forget all about the muck hole, and the heck of a spring we just had
There's no end to feed, so much more than we need and heck it really wasn't that bad!!

Rainy Jane

We had put off processin' the calves, but we couldn't wait no longer
We was well into July them calves were gettin' bigger and stronger

Those calves was growin', gettin' harder to handle with each passin' day
There'd been nothin' but rain, rain, and more rain since way back in May

The workin' pens had all dried up but didn't stay that way for long
We thought we'd picked a good day but found out we were wrong

Leonard came to help, brought along Jane from Scotland too
It sure didn't take Jane long, 'fore she found a job to do

I was vaccinatin', while she was loadin' the taggin' gun
We was all complainin' while Jane was havin' fun

At first, it was just showers, then it turned to pourin' rain
We were almost drowned, but you couldn't wipe the smile off Jane

One thing about foreign folks, they think it's all just grand
They're wantin' a "Canadian Experience" these folks from another land

She was havin' the time of her life, just imagine the stories she'd tell
To her, she was livin' the "Canadian dream", to us, it was a livin' hell!!

Winter 2018

Leonard MacCuish has been our "right hand man" for years. Jane Melrose was a foreign visitor who came along to help us out a few times that summer, moving cattle and even to endure that memorable day we all got soaked.

Ranchin's a Gamble

I'm layin' on the couch, I ain't havin' too much fun
felt like I coughed up a lung but, I managed to get the chores done.

My old feed truck's broke down and It's the coldest time of the year
It's -32 and droppin' and I'm a-feedin' with the open-air John Deere

Now, this wouldn't be my choice, especially when I'm feelin' this way
But, cows eat every day of the week, Rancher's don't get no sick day

No Rancher's Union to tell us it's too cold to feed today
In fact, the more the mercury drops, the more Ol' Bossy needs her hay

No Payday every 2 weeks, nope, we only get paid when we sell
and what them critters might bring, well, you never can tell

We can't control the market, we haul 'em in and take what we get
The gross looks pretty awesome, but, not when you look at the net

It sure ain't for the weak of heart, you gotta have nerves of steel
If you like the monthly payment plan, ranchin' sure ain't yer deal

Our lives depend on the weather and what Mother Nature decides to do
And watchin' your dreams fade with the frost can tear the heart out of you

You gotta be willin' to risk it all, to lay it all on the line
Heck!, We don't have to go to "Vegas", Ranchin's a gamble all the time

Makin' Fence

Today we're goin' fencin'. It ain't the job I like the most
I'll be drivin' the tractor and Larry'll be poundin' the posts

"Just drive beside the wire" he says, but I'm always too close or too far
As if them cows could really care less just where them fence posts are

If I was the one pounding the posts, it wouldn't matter to me
If I was off a tad here or there, as long as I was in the right vicinity

I'd whap them suckers in the ground, and nail the wire to it.
Ya think If the post is 6 inches too far North the cows will go right thru it?

If he goes to pound a post, and a rock is in the way,
I swear It's a National disaster, like it ruins his whole dang day

He's too particular, but when he's done, the fence posts are all just so
It surely does look nice, all right, when they're in a perfect row

And there's exactly 5 paces between each post, precise right to the letter
I doubt there's anyone around could make a fence look any better

I guess it's good that he's so fussy, 'cause if you left it up to me
I'd probably say to heck with the posts I'd nail the wire to a tree.

Mother Nature's Dance

Yesterday, we were greeted by a foot of snow
And we were sure convinced that it would never go

Now today, I'm feedin' cows in the freezin' rain
and ice and sleet and snow and I hate to complain

but, when I was finally done, I was soakin' wet and froze
I was startin' to rethink this here Ranchin' life we've chose

We can't put off doin' chores for a nicer day
Each day we face the elements and take it come what may

Where is the "good life" part? Where is the romance??
We cannot choose the music, but we have to dance the dance

to the tune of Mother Nature's choice while she decides our fate
One thing's for sure Y'all don't pay enough for that steak there on your plate

October 2016

MY OLD 1969 INTERNATIONAL

I'm pickin' up on the fly; the old truck's a-gurglin' and a-hissin'
I figure I need me three eyes just to maintain my position.

One to stay fixed on that place on the tractor tire,
One to watch the temperature gauge rising higher and higher,

And one to watch Larry givin' me directions for further and closer,
I figure keepin' this ol' gal a-runnin' is the best we can hope fer.

She started to run hot, so a jug of water I found
I poured it all in and then watched it all run on the ground

And this sure ain't the worst of her problems, I might add
But the last straw might be this hole in her rad

The key won't work unless you get it just right
And the split-shift quit workin' some time late last night

She'll lock up solid in reverse and first gear
And she moans and groans in bull-low it's frightful to hear

When she's in 2nd and 5th, She's sure to jump out
And She wanders a tad when you get'er wound out

But 3rd and 4th they work just fine
In my old International 1969.

Most of the lights and the gauges don't work like they should
The clutch is shot and the brakes, well, they ain't that good

The windows don't work and the door handle's broke
You gotta reach around with your finger and give it a poke.

My Larry, he claims I'm the only one that would drive her
threatens to cut'er in half, the box and hoist would be the survivor

But I love that old truck, even though I know it's absurd
She has been a dandy but "has been" is the operative word.

This might be the first poem I ever wrote before I knew there was such a thing as "Cowboy Poetry"

OUTSIDE THE BOX

Thinkin' outside the Box

"My Larry" is an entrepreneur there really is no doubt
His many schemes have got us thru' tough times like *BSE and the drought.

But this time he's out on a limb, where only "My Larry" would go
We had a quarter that was too dry to seed, so it ended up summer fallow

We was in a midst of a drought, no pasture and even less hay
mid-July it started to rain and that summer fallow just plumb got away

He finally got a chance to work it down, but then he changed his mind
There was a fine crop of wild oats a-growin', better feed you just can't find

Then he decided to take it one step further, as "My Larry" will often do
Since there was still rain in the forecast, he decided to fertilize it too

"My Larry" sure thinks outside the box, not many folks would fertilize a weed
But hay was in short supply and wild oats makes good feed

That crop went 4 bales per acre and we got 85 bucks for each bale of hay
And we cleaned up all the wild oats, thinkin' outside the box really does pay

August 2015

*BSE (Bovine Spongiform Encephalitis) or Mad cow disease, decimated the Canadian Beef Industry from 2003 – 2011.

I'd rather be in the Saddle

It's great to have abundant feed, only a fool would disagree
But a bumper crop of hay is really not the best news for me

'Cause you see all them bales of hay, they don't come home on their own
Larry's balin' or workin' down stubble so, I do most of the haulin' alone.

On them beautiful fall days, If we only knew just how long it would last
One might take time off for a ride, but that weather can change really fast

And I'd rather haul before the snow, it's much easier that's for sure
But wastin' my fall in a tractor cab is almost more than I can endure

When you complain that the price is too high, You folks who buy your hay
Stop and think where your seat has been on many a glorious fall day

I reckon your seat's been in the saddle some, right where I wish mine had bin
Instead of spendin' all fall in a tractor seat, day out and day in

Don't complain about the price of Hay!!!

When you complain that the price is too high, You folks who buy your hay
Just think what you do all summer and fall, so I guess now you have to pay

I watch the horse trailers and campers go by on many a glorious day
We spend all our time puttin' up feed, while you have time to play

We have some real fine ranch horses, but we seldom ride for fun
When you're ranchin' and raisin' cattle there's too much work to be done

You have no land or equipment payments, no costs for fuel or repair
When supplies are low and prices high, you're cryin' 'bout how it ain't fair

What ain't fair is when feed is scarce, Mother Nature is to blame
Our hay yields are reduced, but input costs are the same

It's all about supply and demand, the bills don't go away
We just get what the market will bear, and you will just have to pay

You accuse us of being greedy – we're taking advantage of the situation
Why not stockpile when feed is cheap and not buy out of desperation

I reckon I'm a charitable person, some of you wouldn't likely agree
I'm willing to help my fellow man, but, you won't get no cheap hay from me.

2019

No Place for the Ranch

Our kids can both ride and it fills us with pride 'cause we taught them all that we know
On a horse or the ground, they're the best help around our efforts really do show

The kid's horses were gems and they worked well for them now they're knockin' on heaven's door
The kids are both grown they've got lives of their own they ain't 'round to help much no more

They've both got big plans, there's no place for the Ranch on the trails that they choose to roam
Still, I think back to a time and I'd give all that is mine if their trails would lead them back home

We're gettin' long in the tooth, that's the cold hard truth our bodies are achin' and sore
His shoulders are gone, I ain't got a leg to stand on and we wonder what we're workin' for

We should sell half the herd, it's really absurd to run as many cows as we do
Still it's hard to let go tho' we have to we know, 'cause there's just too much work for us two

It's hard to understand the kids ain't tied to the Land not like their father and I
They've both got big plans there's no place for the Ranch but, our memories will never die

August 2015

Our Son, Landon, has since joined us on the Ranch. We are so thankful that he has found a place for the Ranch in his life and I feel so blessed to be able to work with "my Larry" and our son.

Our Legacy

I'm haulin' hay from the River, tho' why I just don't know
You see we sold the "River Land" about 3 years ago

We decided to downsize, sold the land furthest away
Yup! We sold that the "River Land", but we still make the hay

And with the proceeds from the sale, we bought some more hay land
Somehow, this here downsizin' sure ain't workin' like I planned

We talk 'bout cuttin' back, but, keep accumulatin' more
More land, more cows, way more work what do we need more for?

But wait! our son has come back home, He's here to take it on
The Ranch, our Legacy, shall live long after we are gone

He dreams of buyin' more land and runnin' way more cattle
I dream of slowin' down and leisure time in the saddle

I s'pose I'm not that stoved up, got a few years in me yet
To watch our dreams continue, how much better can it get?

Survival of the Fittest

I know that Nature is cruel and "survival of the Fittest" always prevails
For, I watch that fight for existence all day while I'm haulin' bales

It's not the courageous fight to the death between the wolf pack and the mighty Moose
it's the stuggle between those big ugly Ravens and the tiny defenseless field Shrews

I lift the bales and watch the drama unfold right there before my eyes
The Hunter waits for his chance to attack while the Hunted run for their lives

I know they chew the twines and wreck the bales and they are NOT welcome in my house
Still, deep down in my heart of hearts, I'm always cheerin' for the cute little Mouse!!

Mix Mill Drill

One mornin' I had a dentist appointment to replace a crown
the phone rang, the line was dead, I almost put it down

Then I heard Larry very clearly "can you hear me now?"
"I'm inside the mix mill, check on me before you leave for town"

He forgot his torn rotator cuff when he climbed inside that thing.
Wasn't sure he could hoist himself out with only "one good wing"

I said "sure", but got distracted, and off to town I went
Forgettin' about "My Larry" and his predicament

My face was froze, Dr. Bud was busy workin' with his drill
When I recalled my Larry could still be stuck in the mix mill

Then he called me on my cell, and he did not sound too happy
Said I better get back home and I better make it snappy

Well, I could not reply, 'cause They was workin' on my tooth
And there wasn't much that I could do to tell the honest truth

I couldn't speak but made some sound into my cell phone
I think he kinda got the message, that he was on his own

I'm not sure how the story went, he never spoke of it agin
Perhaps he learnt to be sure he can get out before he decides to get in!

Who the heck is "Roy"

I went to check the horses after the storm went through
Brought them a bale of hay, seemed like the least that I could do

They're winterin' on a Quarter just a half a mile away
The place is known as "Roy's" though why, no one can say

Is it just me? Doesn't anyone else find it kinda' funny?
No one recalls who this "Roy" guy was, not for love nor money

It's common with tracts of land, and I've always found it strange
No matter who owns the land, the name will never change

Many times I went to the wrong place, when I was a new bride
I couldn't keep all the names straight, no matter how hard I tried

There's Roy's and Phillip's and Jakes and Peter's and Paul's and Joe's
And a Ranch just a mile South of us that has always been Gramboe's

There's Eli's and Martin's and Mabel's and Prudat's and Frank's and Fred's
And a half-section we've owned for 25 years and alas! It's still called Ted's

It's a tribute to the homesteaders, to the spirit of the Pioneer
But, I often wonder, after we're gone, will anyone know we were here??

March 2017

Nature's Restoration (A new perspective)

I rode my golden boy today, perhaps, to ease my troubled mind
Perhaps to gain a new perspective, perhaps to leave my life behind

The trail's been mighty rough these days, there's just no place to hide
When my soul seeks restoration, It's time for me to ride

I used only a halter, saw no need for other tack
sometimes I need to "feel" my horse, so I chose to ride bareback

We checked the horses out on "Roy's", a half mile to the East
The field we crossed was pristine white untouched by Man or Beast

The powdered snow was soft and deep above my Wiley's knees
The sun's rays sparkled 'cross the landscape and shimmered in the trees

As hooves disturbed the virgin surface, Icy crystals sprayed
They danced and shone like diamonds glist'nin' from the tracks we made

We entered a tiny forest trail flanked by aspen, then, thick pines
a canopy hides the forest floor where the sun it never shines

My spirit soothed, my soul restored, Mother Nature softly caressed
She wrapped me in her loving arms and I felt truly blessed

We are the few who choose to live in this unspoiled space
With God's wild and wondrous creatures, we share this perfect place

I gained a new perspective, we are just part of the "Master's Plan"
Our place is to keep the faith and just do the best we can.

January 12, 2019

Larry and Choco 2019

A Stroke of Luck

When we go to check the cows, it's become quite a joke
'Cause I do all the driving, now that "My Larry's" had a stroke

See, the one in the passenger seat gets the job everyone hates
The feller ridin' "shotgun" gets to open all the gates

I must take advantage of this situation the best way that I can
No doubt, when He's back behind the wheel, it'll be my job again

Now, if you didn't know he had a stroke, you probably couldn't tell
The only real deficit is he don't recall so well

Sooooooo, I managed to convince him he that he loves to clean the house
This stroke is really workin' for me, I now have the perfect spouse

Now, he's busy dustin', sweepin' and moppin' all the floors
Doin' all the inside jobs I hate, while I'm outside doin' chores

He's cookin' up a storm, fact, he took over my kitchen
And that's just fine with me, I sure ain't doin' any b... complainin'

Told him he was a pro with the washer and the dryer
"My Larry" never did no laundry, I am a big fat liar

Things was goin' mighty fine, reckon I had the perfect life
all a rancher really needs is a good hardworkin' wife

Then, I mentioned cleaning toilet bowls, said he was the only one I trusted
If looks could kill, I'da died right there, I knew that I was busted

This poem is mostly fictional, not too much of it is true
But if you can find some humour, it will help to get you through.

August 2019

Snake's Hips

I mixed up the concoction and I fired it past my lips
It went down nice and easy, smooth like rattlesnake's hips

I'd called a cowpoke friend of mine 'cause he knew what to do
He often used this remedy, so it was tried and true

10 cc's of penicillin mixed in a glass of Juice
I had a good supply on hand, meant for livestock use

You see, I was in a pickle, I was flyin' out real soon
to the Kamloops Gathering, but I couldn't carry a tune

There was no time to see the Dr., so I really had no choice
This was my first big "gig", I couldn't afford to lose my voice

So....I mixed up the concoction and I fired it past my lips.
It went down nice and easy, smooth like rattlesnake's hips

2019

I am very fortunate to have my daughter, Lacey, for a "Roadie". We have so much fun travelling together

Christmas Diamonds for a Cowgal

It was in the winter of 2002 cattle prices were way down
To supplement our cash flow, I worked at an office in town

It was Christmas and I was 'bout as happy as a cowgal could be
'Cause on Christmas mornin', I found Diamonds underneath the tree

They were somethin' I'd always wanted and "My Larry" had spared no expense
I ranted and raved to my co-workers 'til they could barely stand the suspense

It became a bit of a game, as everyone tried to guess
Was it earrings, a bracelet, a necklace? But I would not confess

I hosted the Christmas party that year we all had so much fun
I didn't bring out my "surprise" diamonds 'til all the festivities were done

Finally, I placed the box on the table, tryin' hard to conceal my grin
Then, I slowly lifted the lid to reveal the "Diamond" HOOF NIPPERS within!!

Dec 2014

Printed in the United States
by Baker & Taylor Publisher Services